DiscoverRoo
An Imprint of Pop!
popbooksonline.com

Living through American History

Living through the CIVIL WAR

by Grace Hansen

WELCOME TO DiscoverRoo!

This book is filled with videos, puzzles, games, and more! Scan the QR codes* while you read, or visit the website below to make this book pop.

popbooksonline.com/civil-war-life

abdobooks.com

Published by Pop!, a division of ABDO, PO Box 398166, Minneapolis, Minnesota 55439.

Printed in the United States of America, North Mankato, Minnesota.

052023
092023

THIS BOOK CONTAINS RECYCLED MATERIALS

Cover Photo: Getty Images
Interior Photos: Getty Images, Library of Congress; Shutterstock Images
Editor: Elizabeth Andrews
Series Designer: Laura Graphenteen; Neil Klinepier

Library of Congress Control Number: 2022950516

Publisher's Cataloging-in-Publication Data

Names: Hansen, Grace, author.
Title: Living through the Civil War / by Grace Hansen
Description: Minneapolis, Minnesota : Pop!, 2024 | Series: Living through American history | Includes online resources and index
Identifiers: ISBN 9781098244309 (lib. bdg.) | ISBN 9781098245009 (ebook)
Subjects: LCSH: United States--History--Civil War, 1861-1865--Juvenile literature. | United States--Politics and government--19th century--Juvenile literature. | Social history--Juvenile literature.
Classification: DDC 973.2--dc23

*Scanning QR codes requires a web-enabled smart device with a QR code reader app and a camera.

TABLE OF CONTENTS

CHAPTER 1

THE CIVIL WAR

In 1860, Abraham Lincoln was elected President of the United States. He had a vision to free enslaved people whose family members were brought to North America generations before.

Agriculture was the largest industry in the South. Southern plantations

WATCH A VIDEO HERE!

Abraham Lincoln was the 16th President of the United States.

relied heavily on the labor of enslaved people who did nearly all the farm work, including most other household duties.

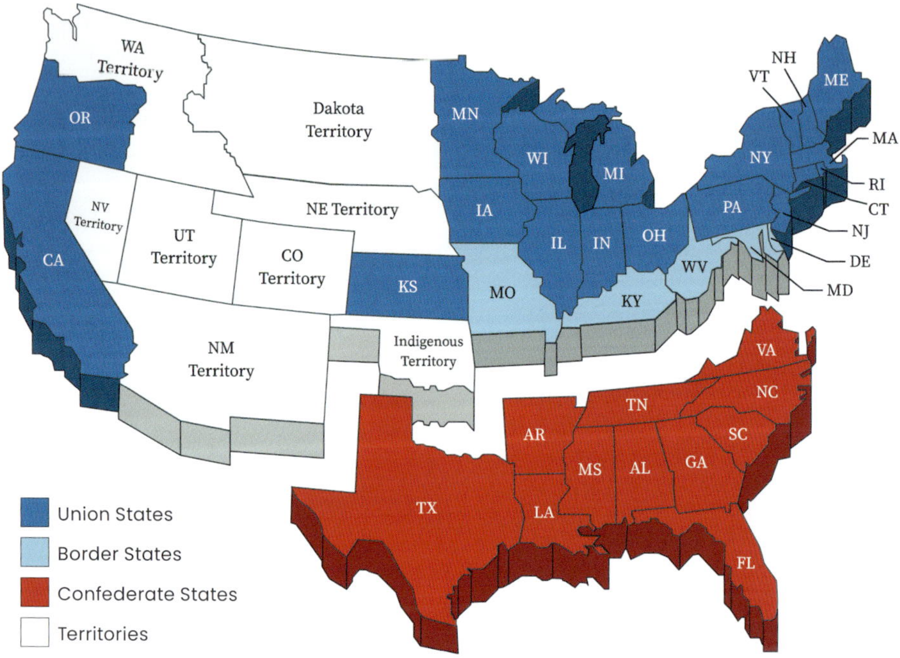

President Lincoln would put an end to slavery. To keep life the same, Southern states chose to leave the Union. Lincoln was determined to keep the country whole, even if it meant war.

The Civil War began on April 12, 1861. Union states fought Confederate states.

Border states were slave states that did not leave the Union. It was a time of great change for the entire country. Many men left home to fight. Civilians had to work even harder.

The Emancipation Proclamation legally freed 3.5 million enslaved people.

CHAPTER 2

LIFE AS A CIVILIAN

During this time, factories in Northern cities had plenty of jobs. But most Northerners lived in rural areas. Families in these areas farmed the land. Many farmers left to fight in the war. The others worked overtime to feed Northerners throughout the war years.

LEARN MORE HERE!

Women's work in munitions factories during the Civil War was very important.

Most of the war took place in the South. Union forces blocked many Southern **ports**. This was a **tactic** to stop food and other necessities from reaching Southern civilians. Many went hungry.

Women took on more responsibilities. In addition to caring for households, women also tended to businesses formerly run by men. Women also began wearing more **practical** work clothing, such as pants. Those who had time for social activities gathered to stitch quilts and discuss the war.

Meanwhile, most children were educated in schoolhouses. One teacher taught local

RICHMOND BREAD RIOT

On April 2, 1863, a crowd of more than 100 women gathered in Richmond, Virginia. They marched with their weapons and chanted, "Bread or blood!" Hundreds more joined them. The mob broke into the government **storehouses** and took what they could get.

children of all ages. Once students learned reading and writing, many went straight to work. Others went on to schools to study special trades. Academies for students ages 13 to 20 offered lessons on chemistry, philosophy, and other subjects.

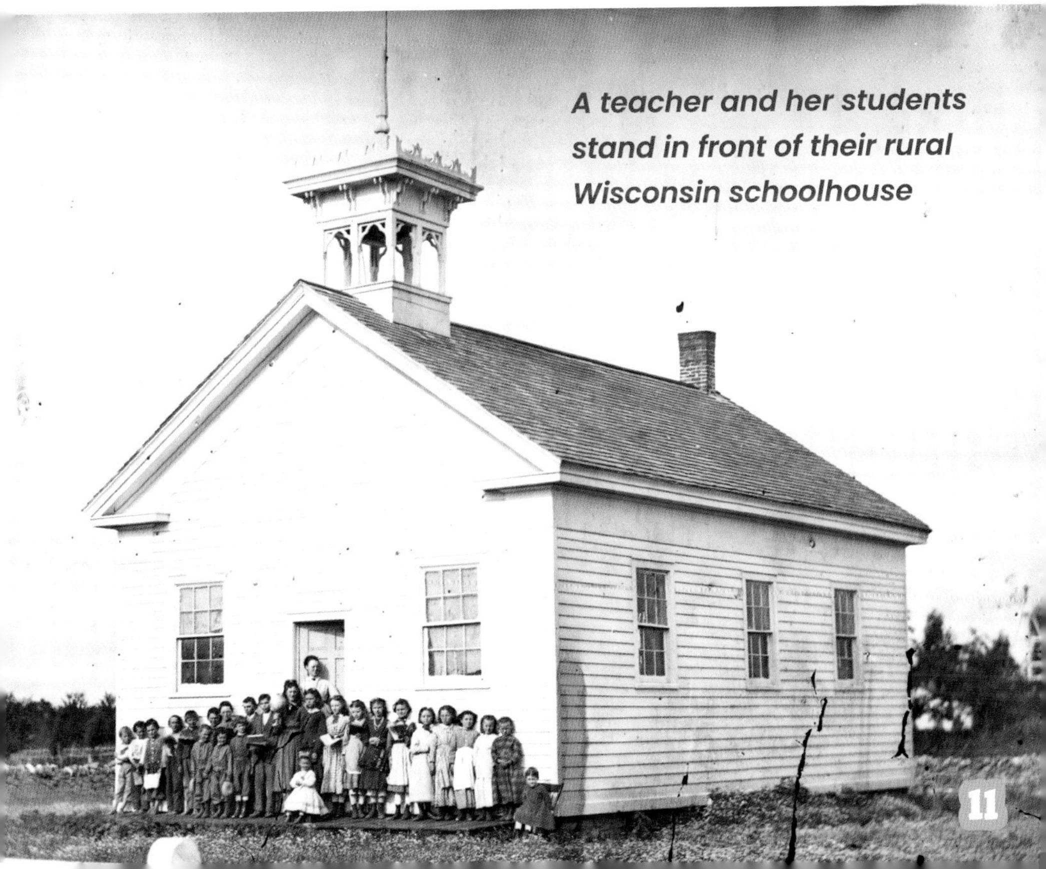

A teacher and her students stand in front of their rural Wisconsin schoolhouse

CHAPTER 3

LIFE AS AN ENSLAVED PERSON

While the Union and **abolitionists** fought for enslaved people's freedom, enslaved people were forced to continue working. Life as an enslaved person in the South was very hard. Most worked for hours in hot fields. Others worked as cooks, maids, and nannies.

EXPLORE LINKS HERE!

There were more than 45,000 plantations in the South in 1860. About half had a workforce of up to 30 enslaved people.

Enslaved people often lived together in cabins with dirt floors and no windows. Weekly food was delivered to the cabins for breakfast and dinner. Lunch was served in the fields. Clothing made of poor materials were handed out at the start of each year. By the year's end, the clothes had turned to rags.

Housing for the enslaved commonly slept eight to ten people.

One of the harshest parts of slavery was the separation of families. Children of enslaved people were property of their owners and could be sold away at any time. This was **traumatic**. But enslaved people were rarely allowed to show emotion without being punished.

This illustration depicts an enslaved father being sold away from his family.

DID YOU KNOW?

Lincoln issued the Emancipation Proclamation on January 1, 1863. It declared that "all persons held as slaves are, and henceforward shall be free."

CHAPTER 4

LIFE AS A SOLDIER

Soldiers dealt with hunger, miles of walking, poor weather conditions, and the possibility of death. In fact, by the end of the war, 620,000 men had lost their lives. Black soldiers accounted for 40,000 of those deaths.

COMPLETE AN ACTIVITY HERE!

These tent-shaped graves of soldiers in City Point, Virginia, helped prevent rain water from seeping through the dirt. Later, two slabs of concrete would be added atop each mound.

The Union army received the services of nearly 180,000 freed and escaped enslaved people. Even though they were in the North, Black soldiers still struggled to receive equal treatment. Racist

Black men belonging to the 107th Regiment pose at Fort Corcoran in Arlington, VA.

stereotypes were to blame. And yet the men continued to prove themselves on the battlefield. They became known among the entire Union army as fierce and strong fighters.

By the war's end, Black soldiers had fought in almost 450 battles. Their service and sacrifice were essential in a Union victory.

Soldiers began their mornings with military drills. They learned to fight as a unit and respond to officer commands. More drills followed in the afternoons. In between, the men cooked meals and tended to their clothing and weapons.

An officer sits on a box of hardtack. Hardtack is a hard cracker that soldiers relied on for food.

CIVIL WAR ERA HARDTACK RECIPE

INGREDIENTS

- 2.5 cups flour
- 1/2 cup water
- 1 tsp salt

DIRECTIONS

- Mix flour and salt
- Begin adding water in small amounts, about ¼ at a time, while kneading
- If it's very sticky, add a bit more flour one tablespoon at a time
- Mold the dough into a ball
- Roll out the dough
- Using a knife, cut the dough into squares
- Poke holes in the crackers using a fork or skewer
- Bake at 375 degrees for 30 minutes or until edges begin to brown
- Let cool completely before eating

In their free time, soldiers socialized by playing games or singing songs together. They also wrote letters to loved ones.

Confederate soldiers play a game of poker at their campsite as two enslaved men serve them food and drink.

Injured Union soldiers recover at the Armory Square Hospital in Washington D.C.

After battle, wounded soldiers greatly outnumbered doctors. Wounds to the middle of the body were hard to treat. Wounded arms and legs were often cut off. Those who survived their injuries risked dying from **infection**. Many others died of disease.

President Lincoln was killed in April 1865. He was never able to see the United States restored.

President Andrew Johnson declared a formal end to the Civil War in August of 1866. By then, the country and its people were in the time known as the Reconstruction era. Soldiers returned to their homes and jobs. Southerners faced a new system of labor.

Black Americans had freedoms and new rights, such as voting. Some began to hold public office. Many older Black Americans got an education for the first time in their lives. Although there was much work to be done, the Civil War opened new paths for the young country. Many Americans began paving the way toward a better future for every person.

Hiram Revels was elected by the Mississippi legislature to the US Senate during the Reconstruction era. He was the first Black person to serve in either house of US Congress.

A DAY IN THE LIFE

Nathan is a Civil War Union soldier with the 10th Indiana Volunteer Infantry Regiment. He has been serving for nearly three years.

6:00AM

Nathan and the other soldiers wake before dawn. The men prepare breakfast. It seems the weather will be warm and pleasant.

6:30AM

Normally, it would be time to start drills. But today the men had marching orders. They begin to pack up camp. Nathan carefully packs his belongings, including his Bible and letters from home.

7:00AM

Nathan and the soldiers begin the march. Luckily, today's march would be better than others. Some days the men walked 25 miles (40km). Today the walk would be just 10 miles (16km).

12:00PM

Nathan looks behind him as he walks. Soldiers stretched for miles. Some were singing. Injured soldiers had a tougher time. Horses and mules pulled large cannons.

1:00PM

The soldiers walk alongside a thick forest. Nathan and others stop to tap the trees for resin. The surgeon will make **turpentine** from the resin to treat wounds.

7:00PM

The men had finished the march and set up camp. Dinner was cleaned up. A group wanted to play poker. It was a night to celebrate. Rumor came that General Joseph E. Johnston was close to surrender. Nathan was too excited to play poker. He went to his tent to write a letter home.

MAKING CONNECTIONS

TEXT-TO-SELF

Imagine you are living during the Civil War. What are your daily routines? How has your life changed?

TEXT-TO-TEXT

Have you read any other books about life during the Civil War? What information was the same in each book? What information was different?

TEXT-TO-WORLD

How might the United States look today if the American Civil War never happened?

GLOSSARY

abolitionist — a person who supported abolition, or the ending of slavery, before the Civil War.

infection — an illness caused by germs.

port — a place where ships load and unload, and its nearby town or city.

practical — fitting the needs of a particular situation in a helpful way.

stereotype — a common, over generalized, and inaccurate belief about a particular group of people.

storehouse — a building or space where goods are stored.

tactic — a technique or maneuver used for achieving a goal, especially in battle.

traumatic — an emotional shock that has a deep effect on one's life.

turpentine — a mixture of oil and resin from certain trees. Civil War surgeons sometimes used this on the sick and injured, believing it to be helpful. However, ingestion was often toxic. Harsh side effects were common.

INDEX